THE GREATEST
INVENTIONS
OF ALL TIME

Jillian Powell

WAYLAND

First published in paperback in 2016 by Wayland
Copyright © Wayland, 2016
All rights reserved.

Dewey Number: 600-dc23

Printed in China

ISBN: 978 0 7502 9780 6
Library ebook ISBN: 978 0 7502 9545 1
10 9 8 7 6 5 4 3 2 1

Wayland
An imprint of Hachette Children's Group
Part of Hodder & Stoughton
Carmelite House
50 Victoria Embankment
London EC4Y 0DZ

An Hachette UK Company
www.hachette.co.uk
www.hachettechildrens.co.uk

Editor: Elizabeth Brent
Designer: Elaine Wilkinson
Researchers: Hester Vaizey and Edward Field
at The National Archives

The National Archives, London, England.
www.nationalarchives.gov.uk

The National Archives looks after the UK government's historical documents. It holds records dating back nearly 1,000 years from the time of William the Conqueror's Domesday Book to the present day. All sorts of documents are stored there, including letters, photographs, maps and posters. They include great Kings and Queens, famous rebels like Guy Fawkes and the strange and unusual – such as reports of UFOs and even a mummified rat!

Disclaimer: Every effort has been made to trace the copyright holder but if you feel you have the rights to any images contained in this book then please contact the publisher.

Please note:
The website addresses (URLs) included in this book were valid at the time of going to press. However, because of the nature of the Internet, it is possible that some addresses may have changed, or sites may have changed or closed down since publication. While the author and publishers regret any inconvenience this may cause to the readers, no responsibility for any such changes can be accepted by either the author or the publishers.

Contents

Incredible inventions

The greatest inventions change people's lives forever. Imagine life without the option to ride your bicycle, or travel by car, train or plane. Think what the world would be like without radio, television or the Internet. Many of the most revolutionary inventions have become part of our everyday lives, and we now take them for granted. For example, it is only when there is a power cut that we can imagine how shadowy and dark life was, before the invention of electric lighting.

The most incredible inventions can come from humble beginnings, or great catastrophes. The printing press, which changed the world in 1439 because it meant books could be printed over and over again, rather than laboriously handwritten, was modelled on wooden olive and wine presses used in the Mediterranean. The aeroplane was developed during World War I, for use in spy and bombing missions, but went on to make overseas travel fast and affordable. Wars often lead to new discoveries and inventions.

Some inventions go back further than you might think, too. Did you know that the Romans invented concrete and under-floor heating, or that wigs were invented in Ancient Egypt?

This book looks at the amazing people and incredible stories behind some of the greatest inventions of all time, and at how they went on to change the world.

Inventors can risk their lives carrying out dangerous experiments to develop their idea. Some have even been killed by their own inventions, such as Horace Lawson Hunley, who invented the first combat submarine but died when it sank on a test mission.

Down on the farm

In 1701, an inventor named Jethro Tull created an incredible machine called a seed drill. It became part of a revolution in farming methods and practices known as the Agricultural Revolution. Tull's seed drill used horsepower to mechanize the process of planting seeds, making it more efficient and meaning farmers could produce more food in greater quantities than before!

The seed drill

Jethro Tull was born into a wealthy farming family in Berkshire in 1674. He travelled to Europe to learn about new farming methods. When he returned, he designed a mechanical seed drill, and built the first model using foot pedals from his local church organ. At that time, people sowed seed by hand, and it was often wasted, or fell unevenly, making it difficult to weed between plants as they grew.

A portrait of Tull, painted around 1720

An engraving of Tull's design for the seed drill

The seed drill sowed faster and more efficiently, and meant that the plants grew in straight rows. The machine had a plough at the front to cut straight furrows into the soil at the right depth. The seeds passed through a funnel into the furrow, then a harrow at the back covered them with soil. Three seed drills operating side by side could increase crop production by up to eight times.

A farmer using a more modern seed drill

Mechanizing farming

The seed drill did not change farming overnight. Tull mistakenly believed that soil could provide plants with all the nutrients they needed, and dismissed the idea of fertilizers. The drill was expensive, and could be unreliable. However, by introducing mechanization, it began a revolution in farming methods which ultimately led to the development of the farm machinery we use today, such as tractors, combine harvesters and rotovators. Modern farmers still use seed drills, too, but they look quite different from Tull's original design – and they no longer rely on the foot pedals from dismantled church organs!

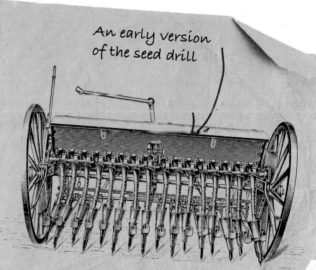

An early version of the seed drill

In the 1960s, a group of British musicians decided to name their band after Jethro Tull! The band was successful for more than 40 years, touring and releasing albums, before splitting up in 2014.

Industrial power

The Industrial Revolution swept through Britain in the 18th and 19th centuries, transforming the country from a rural economy into a manufacturing superpower. It was largely the result of the development of new machinery, including the spinning frame. Created by an inventor named Richard Arkwright in 1768, this revolutionized the production of cotton cloth.

A portrait of Richard Arkwright, painted in 1790

Spinning frame

For centuries, cotton had been hand spun, but the threads were weak and irregular and had to be woven with expensive linen to make strong cloth. Arkwright recruited a clockmaker named John Kay and a team of craftsmen to build a prototype for a spinning frame. It had three pairs of rollers turning at different speeds. As they produced yarn, spindles twisted the fibres together, making a strong, regular thread. Arkwright tried horses, then water wheels, to power the frame. In 1771, he opened a factory next to the River Derwent in Cromford, Derbyshire.

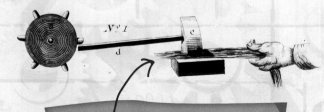

Arkwright's design for a machine to prepare thread for spinning

WANTED AT CROMFORD

FRAMEWORK-KNITTERS AND WEAVERS WITH LARGE FAMILIES.

Likewise children of all ages may have constant employment.

ADVERT IN THE *DERBY MERCURY*, SEPTEMBER 1781.

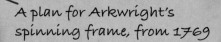

A plan for Arkwright's spinning frame, from 1769

Father of factories

Women and children worked in the spinning factory while weavers worked at home, turning the yarn into cloth. Two-thirds of Arkwright's workers were children, some as young as six. More factories followed in Lancashire, Staffordshire and Scotland, powered by water and later steam, and Arkwright became known as the 'Father of Factories'. Many people criticized Arkwright's invention because it put skilled hand spinners out of work and relied on long hours of child labour. But the fast, cheap production of cotton cloth heralded a new factory age. By 1871, one-third of all the world's cotton cloth was produced in Manchester and the towns and villages surrounding it, and the city was nicknamed 'Cottonopolis'.

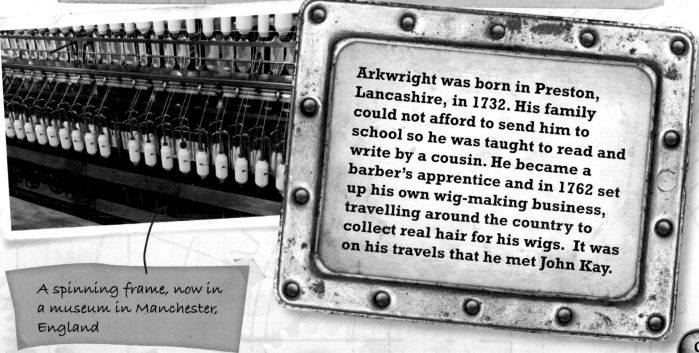

A spinning frame, now in a museum in Manchester, England

Arkwright was born in Preston, Lancashire, in 1732. His family could not afford to send him to school so he was taught to read and write by a cousin. He became a barber's apprentice and in 1762 set up his own wig-making business, travelling around the country to collect real hair for his wigs. It was on his travels that he met John Kay.

Full steam ahead

In the 19th century, the world was changed forever by the invention of steam power. Prior to this, the only transport available was either animal-powered, for example horses and carts, or weather-dependent, such as sailboats. Steam power made it possible for people to travel faster, further, more safely and comfortably, and also made it quicker, easier and cheaper to transport goods around the country.

Trevithick made high-pressure steam 'portable'

The steam engine

Richard Trevithick, born in Cornwall in 1771, was known as 'the Cornish Giant' because he was over 6 feet (1.83m) tall. He became an engineer in the mine where his father worked. Here he began working on the idea of a compact engine, powered by steam under high pressure, that could run on roads or railways. In 1801, he demonstrated a full-sized locomotive, the *Puffing Devil*, taking six friends for a test ride. Although things didn't always go entirely to plan, as the letter below demonstrates, Trevithick's invention of 'strong' or high-power steam meant that compact, portable steam engines could be used in mines, on farms, in factories, on ships and on locomotives.

Trevithick's design for a high-power steam engine

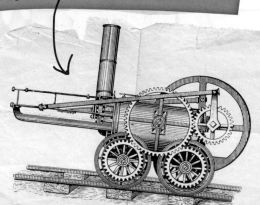

"Yesterday we proceeded on our journey with the engine. We performed the 9 miles in 4 hours and 5 minutes. We had to remove some large rocks on the way. On our return home one of the small bolts that fastened the axle to the boiler broke, and all the water ran out of the boiler."

Letter to Davies Gilbert, February 1804

The passenger railway

George Stephenson was born into a poor family in Wylam, near Newcastle-upon-Tyne, in 1781. Employed as a mechanic in a coalmine, he worked with his son Robert and a friend, Henry Booth, to design and build a steam-powered locomotive that could run on iron rails. *The Rocket* was entered into trials held by the Liverpool and Manchester Railway Company to find the best engine to run between the two cities. On the day of the trials, 15,000 people came to watch the locomotives race. *The Rocket* reached speeds of 24 miles per hour (39 km/h), and was declared the winner.

George Stephenson, painted towards the end of his life

Stephenson's locomotive designs

Reinventing the wheel

The wheel has been around for thousands of years – the earliest depiction of a wheeled wagon is on a pot dating from around 3500–3350 BCE, that was excavated in modern-day Poland. However, three inventors took the wheel and used it as a basis for their own, revolutionary, inventions.

The safety bicycle

John Starley was a gardener's son, born in Essex in 1854. When he was 18, he moved to Coventry to work with his uncle James, who designed bicycles and tricycles. James Starley's designs were an improvement on the earlier 'high wheelers', known as penny-farthings, which had no gears or pedals and gave a bumpy, uncomfortable ride, dangerous at high speeds. In 1885, John designed the first 'safety bicycle', called the 'Rover', which was lighter and cheaper to buy. It made cycling an affordable way to travel for pleasure and sport.

Women racing on penny-farthings in 1891

The safety bicycle had nearly equal-sized wheels

Pneumatic tyres

In 1887, John Boyd Dunlop, a vet working in Belfast, invented an air-filled tyre for his son's tricycle by cutting up an old garden hose and pumping it full of air. Prior to this, tyres were made either from wood or iron, or from solid rubber. Dunlop patented the idea for inflatable rubber tyres, which improved wheel grip on roads, and gave a smoother, safer ride at high speeds. In 1889, he set up the Dunlop business and when a local cyclist, Willie Hume, won a race using the new tyres, they quickly became popular for bicycles and later cars.

Dunlop's son trying out air-filled tyres on his tricycle

The military tank

Sir Ernest Swinton was born in India in 1868, and acted as the government's official war correspondent in World War I. Witnessing trench warfare first hand, he saw soldiers being killed in their thousands by machine gun fire as they advanced towards enemy lines. When he saw tractors pulling guns to the front line, he had the idea of building armoured vehicles running on caterpillar tracks. A "Landships" Committee was appointed to design and build the vehicles in top secret, and the first tank went into battle in 1916. They became important weapons, because they could move over difficult and muddy ground and advance into enemy territory whilst keeping soldiers safe from enemy fire.

Tanks are named after water tanks – when the British Army first began using them on the battlefield, they pretended they were carrying water to the troops, so the enemy wouldn't guess what their brand-new weapons were.

Transforming transport

In the 20th century, three inventions altered transport forever. Two — cat's eyes and the zebra crossing — made Britain's roads dramatically safer. The third — Frank Whittle's jet engine — made travel by air faster and easier than ever before.

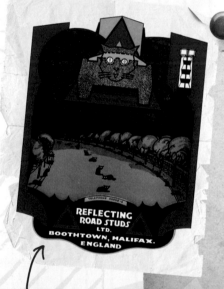

REFLECTING ROAD STUDS LTD. BOOTHTOWN, HALIFAX. ENGLAND

A 1950s book of plans for road studs

Cat's eyes

Percy Shaw left school in Yorkshire in 1903 at the age of 13. He began work repairing roads, using a mechanical roller he built himself from an old engine and lorry wheels. He was driving home one night in 1933, when he saw his headlights reflected in the eyes of a cat by the roadside. He began working on road studs to help guide motorists on dark roads.

Shaw experimented until he reached the design he patented in 1934, opening his own factory in 1935. During blackouts to deter bombing raids in World War II, the British government realised the value of road studs, and soon millions of cat's eyes were being used in Britain and all around the world.

Shaw became famous as an eccentric millionaire inventor, living in a house without curtains, carpets or much furniture, but keeping three televisions running constantly, all with the sound turned down.

Tanks were used to test how robust the studs were

The zebra crossing

Two million cars were using Britain's roads by the 1950s, and road traffic was increasing rapidly. Metal studs and flashing beacons were the only markings for pedestrian crossings and, with road accidents on the rise, the Ministry of Transport carried out trials to find the most effective crossings. The most successful design, the black-and-white striped zebra crossing, was introduced in 1951.

The jet engine

In 1931, Frank Whittle was a 24-year-old fighter pilot with the Royal Air Force when he invented a new kind of aircraft engine. His turbo jet engine replaced pistons and propellers with a rotating gas turbine and air compressor. Whittle struggled to fund his new idea but, in 1937, private sponsors helped him develop the engine, which the Air Ministry adopted after successful test flights. The engine introduced a new jet age, because it made planes much more powerful, and able to travel much more quickly.

A prototype jet engine

Whittle's original design blueprint

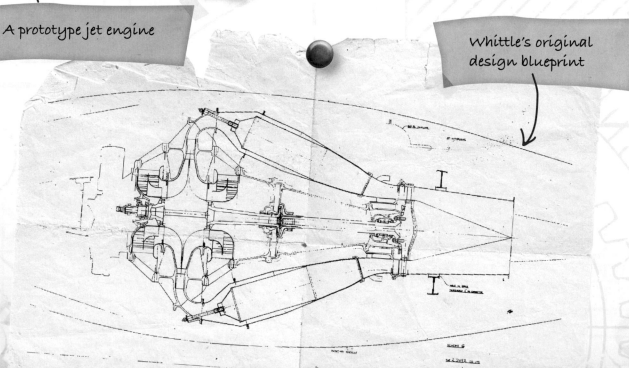

Close to home

Imagine what life would be like if you couldn't turn on an electric light at the flick of a switch, or flush a toilet! From the 18th century onwards, inventions from the light bulb to the vacuum cleaner revolutionized domestic life in Britain.

The flushing toilet

The idea for a flushing toilet developed over centuries. In the ancient civilizations of the Indus Valley and Ancient Rome, running water was used to clear away toilet waste. Queen Elizabeth I's godson, Sir John Harington, designed a water closet for her in 1596 but many people made fun of the idea – preferring to use holes in the ground, or chamber pots! It was not until 1775 that a patent was granted, to a man named Alexander Cummings, for a flushing toilet. Joseph Bramah, a locksmith and cabinetmaker from Yorkshire who installed water closets designed by Cummings, patented an improved design in 1778.

Bramah's other inventions included a beer machine and a hydraulic press

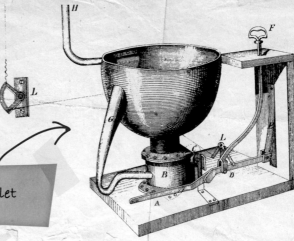

Bramah's 1778 design for a valve toilet

The light bulb

Before electricity, people relied on candles, or gas or oil lamps, for light. A chemist from Sunderland, Joseph Swan, began experiments to create an electric light. He passed electricity through a carbon rod, making it glow inside a sealed glass bulb. In 1878, Swan gave a public demonstration of his lamps in Newcastle-upon-Tyne, but the bulbs only lasted 12 hours and the light was poor. An American scientist, Thomas Edison, improved the design and in 1883, Edison Electric and the Swan Electric Light Company merged to begin manufacturing electric lighting.

Thomas Edison

Joseph Swan at work

The vacuum cleaner

Hubert Cecil Booth, an engineer born in Gloucester in 1871, was watching a train being cleaned by a machine blowing air when he had the idea of a vacuum cleaner that could suck up and contain the dust. Booth's machine replaced dustpans, brushes and carpet beaters but it was so large that the pump, powered by oil and later electricity, had to be pulled on a horse cart. Long hoses ran from the pumps into houses through the door or windows.

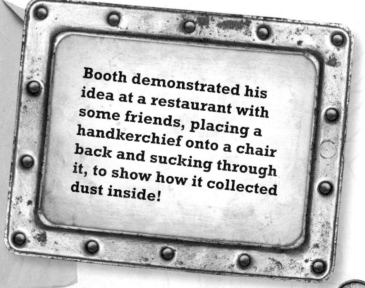

Booth demonstrated his idea at a restaurant with some friends, placing a handkerchief onto a chair back and sucking through it, to show how it collected dust inside!

Easy living

Some inventions have altered domestic life in Britain, making it easier and more comfortable for many people. From the chimney sweeps' rods that meant children no longer had to climb chimneys to sweep them, to the lawnmower, which enabled grass to be cut mechanically, these inventions are still used today.

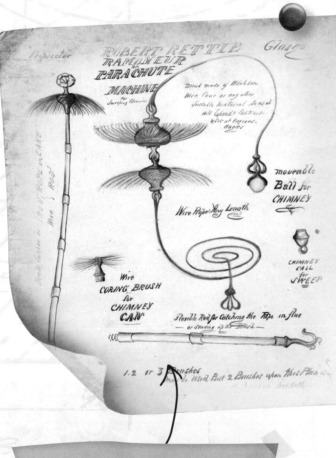

Designs for 'parachute' brushes

Chimney sweeps' rods

As the Industrial Revolution brought coal power to homes and factories, more and more chimneys needed cleaning. Chimney sweeps used small children, aged six or even younger, to climb up inside the chimneys to clean away soot. By the early 1800s, there were calls to replace them with machines. In 1828, Joseph Glass, an engineer from Bristol, improved an earlier idea for a system of canes and brushes, pushed up the chimney through a cloth sleeve.

Chimney sweeps were a common sight in the past

The lawnmower

Edwin Budding was born in Stroud in 1796, and worked as a machinist in a cotton mill. It was a machine there that, in 1830, gave him the idea for a lawnmower. For centuries, grass had been grazed by sheep or cut using hand scythes. Budding's machine made it faster and easier to cut lawns and sports fields. Used together with heavy, cast-iron lawn rollers, it encouraged the Victorian fashion for neat, striped lawns as well as sports such as lawn tennis and croquet.

A woman using an early lawnmower

The toothbrush

William Addis was a London trader who collected rags to sell for papermaking. In 1770, he was imprisoned after being caught up in a street riot, and whilst in prison, he had the idea of making brushes for cleaning teeth. Until then, people used split twigs or rags, and coal dust, soot or salt instead of toothpaste. Addis made his first brush by drilling holes into a meat bone and pushing animal bristles into it. After he was released, he set up a company in 1780, and made his fortune manufacturing toothbrushes. The first mass-produced toothbrushes were made with bone handles and boar bristles or badger hair.

An 18th-century toothbrush

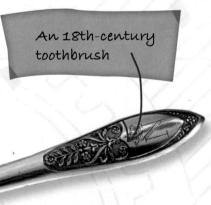

Safe and sound

Clever inventions can be small objects with enormous power. From Humphry Davy's safety lamp, which saved the lives of countless miners, to the hypodermic syringe, which is still used constantly in modern medicine, these inventions were not just life changing, but life saving.

The safety lamp

In 1815, a group of Newcastle miners sent a letter to Sir Humphry Davy, a Cornish chemist and inventor, about the dangers they faced from flammable gases in the coalmines. The candles they wore on their hard hats could spark deadly explosions if they ignited gases such as methane underground. Davy experimented with several models before producing a lamp with a wire mesh around a wick that burned oil. Enough oxygen could reach the flame to keep it alight, but the mesh stopped it from igniting flammable gases.

Davy was knighted in 1812 in recognition of his services to science

Design sketches for the safety lamp

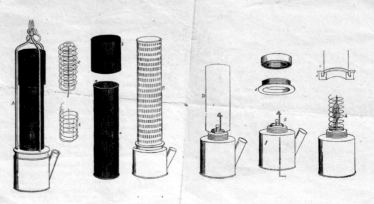

The hypodermic syringe

In 1853, Alexander Wood, a doctor from Edinburgh, used the idea of a bee sting to invent a 'hypodermic' syringe, which had a hollow needle for injecting drugs into the bloodstream. The syringes were at first used for injecting morphine as a painkiller; but their use in medicine was limited due to the lack of injectable drugs available at that time. Today, however, hypodermic syringes are used for everything from blood transfusions to vaccinations and taking blood for blood tests.

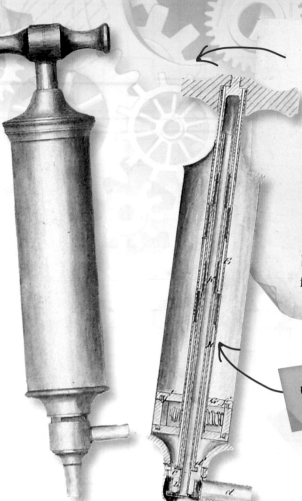

Early syringes were made of metal or glass

The inflatable life jacket

In the 19th century, inventors patented designs for inflatable life preservers, including rings, body vests, armlets and shoes. An American merchant, Peter Markus, invented an inflatable life jacket made from rubberized cloth, with air pockets that could be inflated by pulling a cord to release liquid carbon dioxide from two small cartridges. A fellow American, Andrew Toti, then improved the design using straps to keep the jackets in place. When he died in 2005, he was credited with their invention, until Markus' son wrote to *The New York Times*, giving proof of his father's patents.

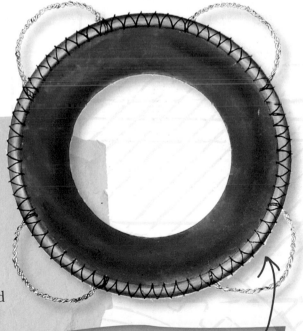

A design for a life buoy from 1845

Food and drink

Inventors and inventions have transformed how, and what, we eat. From contraptions that allow food to be stored for long periods, to devices that keep it hot or cold, our diet today would be very different without them. Some inventions have even resulted in completely new foods, or in the ability to mechanically replicate existing foodstuffs, such as carbonated water.

The tin can

Before the invention of tin cans, food could only be preserved by bottling it in brine, salting and drying it, or potting it with animal fat. In 1810, a British merchant named Peter Durand patented the idea of using tin-coated cans that could be sealed and boiled to sterilize the contents. Canned foods quickly became popular with the Army and Navy and explorers on long expeditions. Durand sold his patent to Bryan Donkin, who began manufacturing canned foods for people to store at home.

The first cans were heavy, and tricky to open

The can opener was not invented for another 40 years after the tin can, and the first cans were so thick they had to be opened with a hammer and chisel!

The vacuum flask

Sir James Dewar, a Scottish chemist and physicist, was working on experiments to cool and liquefy gases when, in 1892, he invented a vacuum flask that could keep liquefied gases at low temperatures. He used two flasks, one inside the other, made from glass painted with reflective metal, with a sealed vacuum between them. This insulated the contents from the outside air temperature, keeping them hot or cold. Dewar failed to patent the idea, and in 1904, the German firm Thermos began manufacturing the flasks for home use, to keep drinks or food hot or cold.

Sir James Dewar, holding one of his vacuum flasks

Carbonated water

People had been drinking naturally occurring carbonated water, where carbon dioxide dissolves in mineral water and makes it fizzy, for thousands of years. However, in 1767, English chemist Joseph Priestley successfully dissolved carbon dioxide in water to make artificially carbonated water. This paved the way for the manufacture of fizzy drinks such as Coca Cola and lemonade.

Joseph Priestley is also credited with the discovery of oxygen

Changing communication

The way we communicate with each other today is constantly evolving with the development of new technology and media, but it was in the 19th century that inventors paved the way for modern methods of communication.

The postage stamp

Writing letters was once the only way that people could stay in touch with each other from a distance. People had to pay for letters when they received them, according to the distance they had travelled and the number of sheets they contained. Some people even tried to cut costs by writing both ways across the paper! In 1839, Rowland Hill, a retired teacher, invented the idea of adhesive postage stamps, to be paid for by the sender, and priced by the weight of the letter. The first stamps were the Penny Black and the Twopence Blue.

Rowland Hill is credited with founding the modern postal service

A Penny Black stamp

Telephone

Sometimes, inventors race against each other to file a patent for the same invention. The Scot Alexander Graham Bell patented his telephone device in 1876, hours before an American, Elisha Gray, applied for a patent. Bell was living in Boston when he made the discovery that sounds could be sent along a wire. Working with Thomas Watson, who was an expert in the new technology of electricity, he found that a wire that connected two springs could carry the sound of vibrations from one spring to the other, in the form of electrical waves. Bell and Watson went on to develop a working model of a telephone and in 1877 set up the Bell Telephone Company.

Alexander Graham Bell

An early wall-telephone

The invention of the telephone triggered the development of the word 'hello' as a greeting.

Instant images

Nowadays, watching television, or taking a picture on a smartphone, is so commonplace that we think nothing of it. So imagine having to rely on an artist's impression to show you what something looks or looked like! Before photography and televisions were invented, drawing, painting or engraving images were the only ways to capture, keep and transmit them.

Fox Talbot at home in Lacock Abbey, in Wiltshire

Photography

William Henry Fox Talbot was an English politician, scientist and inventor. He was on his honeymoon in Italy in 1833 when he had the idea of a light-sensitive machine that could automatically record the scenery he was trying to sketch. In France, the amateur scientists Joseph Niépce and Louis Daguerre had been experimenting with ways of fixing images using light on silver plate, but fixing one image took several hours and the original could not be reproduced.

When he returned home, Fox Talbot began experiments into a way of printing a photographic image on light-sensitive paper using chemicals to produce a 'negative'. This process meant an image could be printed over and over again from the same negative, and was the basis for photography for the next 150 years. It was not overtaken until the development of digital photography in the 1980s.

Examples of cameras through the ages

The television

John Logie Baird was a Scottish engineer, born in 1888. He began inventing when he was still at school, setting up an electric telephone exchange connecting his house with four friends' houses. It had to be dismantled when a low-hanging wire caused a taxi driver to have an accident.

While he was still living in his parents' house, Baird began working on the idea of capturing and transmitting live images, burning his hands during one experiment. In 1923, he managed to create a working television using spare materials including an old tea chest, a hat box and some bicycle light lenses.

Baird became the first person to demonstrate a working model of a television, transmitting black and white images, in 1926. But by 1936, a rival company, Marconi-EMI, introduced a superior electronic system. The following year, the BBC adopted the Marconi system, which was used for nearly 50 years. Although disappointed, Baird went on to experiment with colour and even 3D television.

Early televisions were large and bulky

Clever calculators

Can you imagine a world without computers or the Internet, where the only way of communicating with people was by letter, telephone call, or face-to-face? It seems impossible now, but it was only in the late 20th century that these inventions made the instant global exchange of information and ideas a reality.

A Colossus computer

The Colossus computer

Tommy Flowers was an engineer working with the General Post Office when his research unit was moved to Bletchley Park during World War II. They were given the task of detecting and deciphering secret codes used by the Germans for their war plans. In 1943, he began work on a machine to decipher the German Lorenz code, funding it with his own money. The Colossus machine could read 5,000 characters a minute, and was the world's first electronic, digital and programmable computer. Ten Colossus machines were built, deciphering top-secret information that helped to win the war, but although Flowers had introduced the computer age, the technology remained a military secret for decades.

The World Wide Web

British computer scientist Tim Berners-Lee was working at CERN, the European Physics Laboratory, when he had the idea of using the Internet, a global network of computers, to create the World Wide Web. This involved linking web pages using 'hypertext' – text containing links to other text. This way of linking documents had been used on single computers since the 1960s, but in 1989 Berners-Lee had the idea to link documents on computers around the world, allowing the free and global exchange of information. He created the first live web page in 1991, giving instructions on how to search and post web pages. A new age of invention had arrived.

Tim Berners-Lee speaking at a 2012 conference in the USA

E-mail was invented by a US programmer, Ray Tomlinson, in 1971.

The Internet is run on computers called servers, such as these

29

Glossary

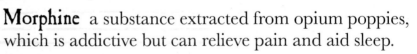

Air compressor a machine that compresses gases to create power.

Blackout turning off all lights, to deter enemy bombing in wartime.

Blueprint a detailed plan or outline.

Boar a kind of wild pig.

Carbon a chemical element.

Deciphering translating a secret code.

Engraving a form of printing created by cutting into wood or metal plate.

Excavated dug out of the ground.

Fertilizer animal manure or chemicals used to feed crops.

Flammable likely to catch fire.

Gas turbine a kind of engine that uses expanding gases to produce thrust.

Laboriously taking a lot of time and hard work.

Linen a type of cloth made from flax plants.

Morphine a substance extracted from opium poppies, which is addictive but can relieve pain and aid sleep.

Nutrient a source of food or nourishment.

Patent the exclusive right to make and use an invention.

Photographic negative an image captured on transparent paper that reverses lights and darks in a scene.

Piston part of an engine, consisting of a cylinder sliding inside a hollow cylinder.

Prototype the original model for a design.

Rotovator a machine for breaking up soil.

Sterilize to kill germs and bacteria.

Trench warfare fighting from deep trenches, as in World War I.

Turbo powered by rotating blades.

Further information

Places to visit

At-Bristol Science Centre, Bristol

Bletchley Park, Milton Keynes

Stephenson's Railway Museum, North Shields

The Museum of Communication, Fife

The National Waterfront Museum, Swansea

The Science Museum, London

W5 Science and Discovery Centre, Belfast

Apps

Design Museum Collection app for iPad
Facts, information and interviews on the design history of the telephone and other important inventions

Journeys of Invention – the Science Museum
Follow interactive journeys through some of the most revolutionary inventions of all time

Pettson's Inventions
A puzzle-type game that challenges players to assemble inventions

Books

How Nearly Everything Was Invented by Brainwaves by Ralph Lazar, Dorling Kindersley, 2008

Illustrated Timeline of Inventions and Inventors by Kremena Spengler, Picture Window Books, 2011

Inventions: A History of Key Inventions That Changed the World by Adam Hart-Davis, Walker Books, 2011

Mistakes That Worked: 40 Familiar Inventions and How They Came to Be by Charlotte Foltz Jones, Doubleday Books for Young Readers, 2013

See Inside: Inventions by Alex Frith, Usborne, 2011

The Story of Inventions by Anna Claybourne, Usborne, 2012

The 10 Greatest Accidental Inventions by Jack Booth, Franklin Watts, 2008

Websites

www.nationalarchives.gov.uk
The website of The National Archives

www.enchantedlearning.com/inventors
An A to Z of inventions, searchable by name or theme, such as science/industry, food or communications

www.factmonster.com/ipka/A0004637.html
An A to Z guide to great inventors and inventions

www.history.com/topics/inventions
Short video clips on inventors and inventions

www.ideafinder.com/history/inventors
A comprehensive website giving facts and myths about great inventions

Index